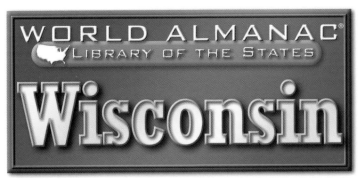

WORLD ALMANAC®
LIBRARY OF THE STATES

Wisconsin

THE BADGER STATE

by Rachel Barenblat

Curriculum Consultant: Jean Craven,
Director of Instructional Support,
Albuquerque, NM, Public Schools

WORLD ALMANAC® LIBRARY

Please visit our web site at: **www.worldalmaclibrary.com**
For a free color catalog describing World Almanac® Library's list of high-quality books
and multimedia programs, call 1-800-848-2928 or fax your request to (414) 332-3567.

Library of Congress Cataloging-in-Publication Data

Barenblat, Rachel.
    Wisconsin, the Badger State / by Rachel Barenblat.
        p. cm. — (World Almanac Library of the states)
    Includes bibliographical references and index.
    Summary: Illustrations and text present the history, geography, people, politics and
government, economy, and social life and customs of Wisconsin.
    ISBN 0-8368-5126-9 (lib. bdg.)
    ISBN 0-8368-5295-8 (softcover)
    1. Wisconsin—Juvenile literature. [1. Wisconsin.] I. Title. II. Series.
F581.3.B35   2002
977.5—dc21
                                                           2001046983

This edition first published in 2002 by
World Almanac® Library
330 West Olive Street, Suite 100
Milwaukee, WI 53212 USA

This edition © 2002 by World Almanac® Library.

Design and Editorial: **Jack&Bill**/Bill SMITH STUDIO Inc.
Editors: Jackie Ball and Kristen Behrens
Art Directors: Ron Leighton and Jeffrey Rutzky
Photo Research and Buying: Christie Silver and Sean Livingstone
Design and Production: Maureen O'Connor and Jeffrey Rutzky
World Almanac® Library Editors: Patricia Lantier, Amy Stone, Valerie J. Weber,
Catherine Gardner, Carolyn Kott Washburne, Alan Wachtel, Monica Rausch
World Almanac® Library Production: Scott M. Krall, Eva Erato-Rudek, Tammy Gruenewald,
Katherine A. Goedheer

Photo credits: p. 4 © PhotoDisc; p. 6 (all) © Corel; p. 7 (top) © Alfred Eisenstaedt/TimePix,
© PhotoDisc; p. 9 © Joseph Sohm/CORBIS; p. 10 © Library of Congress; p. 11 © ArtToday;
p. 12 © Steve Liss/TimePix; p. 13 © Library of Congress; p. 14 © Bettmann/CORBIS; p. 15 (top)
© Hank Walker/TimePix, (bottom) © Richard Hamilton Smith/CORBIS; p. 17 © Richard Hamilton;
p. 18 © David La Haye; Smith/CORBIS; p. 19 © Library of Congress; p. 20 (from right to left)
© PhotoDisc, © Painet, © David La Haye; p. 21 © Painet, © Corel, © Painet; p. 26 (top)
© Christie K. Silver, (bottom) © PhotoDisc; p. 27 (all) © PhotoDisc; p. 29 © Phillip Gould/CORBIS;
p. 30 © Dover Publications; p. 31 courtesy of Wisconsin State Assembly; p. 33 (top) © Library
of Congress, (bottom) courtesy of the Milwaukee Art Museum; p. 34 (top) © Painet, (bottom)
© Library of Congress; p. 35 (all) © Library of Congress; p. 36 © Tom G. Lynn/TimePix; p. 37
© Jason Cohn/TimePix; p. 38 (from right to left) © Bojan Brecell/CORBIS, © Dover Publications;
p. 39 (from right to left) © PhotoDisc, © Library of Congress; p. 40 © Library of Congress; p. 41
(clockwise) © PhotoDisc, © PhotoDisc, © John Swope/TimePix; p. 42–43 © Library of Congress;
p. 44–45 (all) © Corel

Printed in the United States of America

1 2 3 4 5 6 7 8 9 06 05 04 03 02

Wisconsin

In Great Shape

Wisconsin is a state shaped by glaciers. When the glaciers of the last ice age receded, they left boulders, "kettle" potholes, and great lakes in their wake, carving the actual face of the state.

Wisconsin is a state shaped by farming. Much of the land in Wisconsin is rich with nutrients, perfect for growing vegetables and raising animals for both milk and meat. Early inhabitants farmed corn, squash, and beans in Wisconsin; today the state is known for its sweet corn, green beans, cranberries — and especially its dairy farms.

Wisconsin is a state shaped by the people who have lived in it. From its earliest Native inhabitants to the tribes who remain, from the early French fur traders to the melting pot of ethnic groups who call Wisconsin home today, everyone who has lived in Wisconsin has shaped the state. Wisconsin's festivals and fairs celebrate the seasons, the harvest, and the many different cultures. Some people who lived in Wisconsin, such as writer Laura Ingalls Wilder and environmentalist John Muir, founder of the Sierra Club, have also helped shape the state, the country, and the world.

Wisconsin is a state shaped by football — the Green Bay Packers won the first two Super Bowls ever and won again in 1997. Their loyal fans pack the stadium even on the coldest, snowiest days.

Wisconsin is a state shaped by beauty. From the wilderness of the Great Lakes and the north country to the spare, geometric lines of Frank Lloyd Wright's architecture, Wisconsin is filled with beauty.

Wisconsin is a state shaped by history. The French and Indian War, the founding of the Republican and Progressive political parties, the birth of the Sierra Club and the modern environmental movement — these events and more took place in Wisconsin. Read on, and discover all that has shaped Wisconsin and all that Wisconsin has shaped in return.

▶ Map of Wisconsin showing the interstate highway system, as well as major cities and waterways.

▼ Farms in Wisconsin.

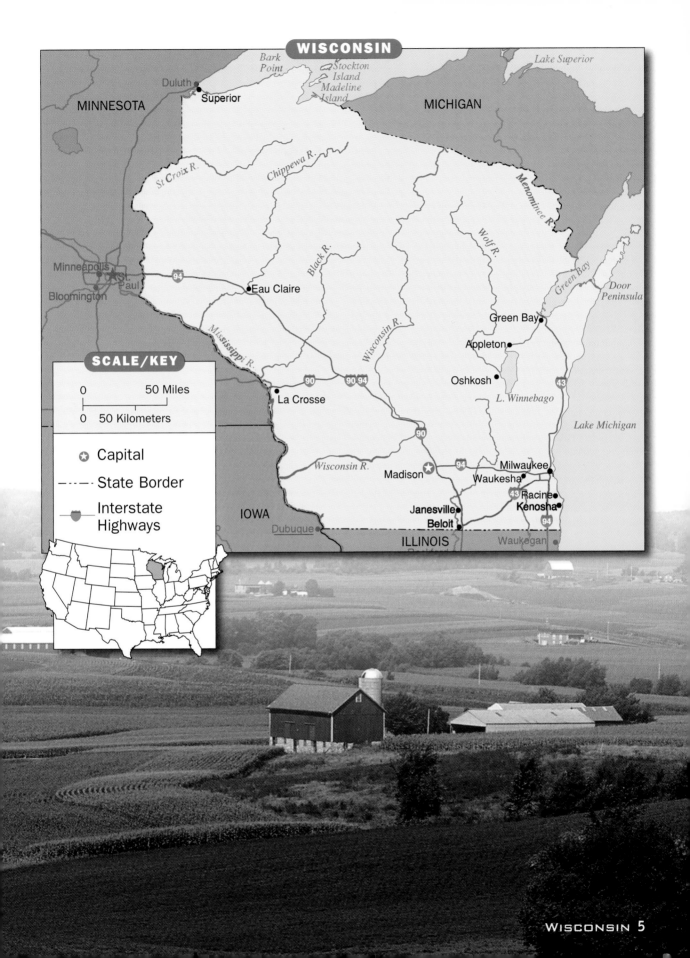

WISCONSIN

Lake Superior

Bark Point

Stockton Island
Madeline Island

MINNESOTA

Duluth
● Superior

MICHIGAN

St Croix R.

Chippewa R.

Menominee R.

Wolf R.

Minneapolis
St. Paul

Bloomington

94

● Eau Claire

Black R.

Green Bay

Door Peninsula

Green Bay ●

Appleton ●

Mississippi R.

Wisconsin R.

Oshkosh ●

43

SCALE/KEY

0 ——— 50 Miles

0 ——— 50 Kilometers

90   90 94

● La Crosse

L. Winnebago

Lake Michigan

⊛ Capital

–·–·– State Border

🛡 Interstate Highways

90

94

Milwaukee ●

Madison ★

Waukesha ●

43 Racine ●

Wisconsin R.

IOWA

Janesville ●

Kenosha ●

Dubuque

Beloit ●

94

ILLINOIS

Rockford

Waukegan ●

Fast Facts

WISCONSIN
1848

WISCONSIN (WI), The Badger State

Entered Union

May 29, 1848 (30th state)

Capital	Population
Madison	208,054

Total Population (2000)

5,363,675 (18th most populous state) — *Between 1990 and 2000, the population of Wisconsin increased by 9.6 percent.*

Largest Cities	Population
Milwaukee	596,974
Madison	208,054
Green Bay	102,313
Kenosha	90,352
Racine	81,855

Land Area

54,310 square miles (140,663 square kilometers) (25th largest state)

State Motto

"Forward"

State Song

"On, Wisconsin!" — *The song was originally the football fight song for the University of Wisconsin at Madison. World-famous bandleader and composer John Philip Sousa proclaimed it the best college song he had ever heard. Fifty years later, in 1959, it was adopted as the state song.*

State Animal

Badger — *The badger is also the mascot of the University of Wisconsin.*

State Bird

Robin — *In 1926–1927, schoolchildren across the state voted the robin as the Wisconsin state bird.*

State Fish

Muskellunge — *The "muskie" is a freshwater fish common to the Great Lakes.*

State Flower

Wood Violet

State Insect

Honeybee

State Tree

Sugar Maple

State Stone

Red granite — *This speckled igneous rock is a common building material.*

State Wildlife Animal

White-tailed Deer

State Domesticated Animal

Cow — *The newest state symbol was adopted in 1993 and reflects the influence of agriculture on Wisconsin's history and culture.*

Wisconsin Dells

Glacially sculpted cliffs rise 100 feet (30 meters) above the water in a region of great natural beauty. In 1856 a reporter concluded "that the wild romantic scenery of the Dells will always make them a place of resort for seekers of pleasure."

The Milwaukee Art Museum, *Milwaukee*

Founded in 1888, the museum today houses collections of European Old Masters, Haitian folk artists, and a collection of decorative arts, including the work of Frank Lloyd Wright.

House on the Rock

During the 1940s Alex Jordan discovered a 60-foot (18-m) chimney of rock in the Wyoming Valley and built a house there called Deer Shelter Rock. Today the fourteen-room house is the core of a complex of many buildings and displays.

For other places and events to attend, see p. 44.

BIGGEST, BEST, AND MOST

- The longest cross-country ski race in North America is the American Birkebeiner. It is 32 miles (52 kilometers) long and covers the distance between the towns of Cable and Hayward.

- Marathon County produces 90 percent of the U.S. supply of ginseng and 10 percent of the world's supply.

- Wisconsin Dells is home to the largest U.S. water-theme park — Noah's Ark.

STATE FIRSTS

- In 1851 the first ice cream sundaes were served in the towns of Manitowoc and Two Rivers.

- The first U.S. hydroelectric plant was constructed at Fox River in 1882.

- Madison is the home of WHA Radio — the world's oldest continuously operating radio station.

Circus Town

In the 1800s Wisconsin was known as the "mother of circuses," and Delavan, Wisconsin, was known as the "circus capital of the nation." Between 1847 and 1894, Delavan was home to twenty-six circuses.

Baraboo, Wisconsin, was the hometown of the Ringling Brothers, who eventually joined forces with their competitor, the Barnum & Bailey Circus.

The Grand Old Party

Several states lay claim to founding the Republican Party, including Wisconsin's neighbors Michigan and Illinois. The first meetings took place in 1854 as Michigan members of the Whig and Free Democratic Parties expressed their opposition to slavery and, around the same time, a meeting was held in Ripon, Wisconsin, to protest the Kansas–Nebraska Bill, which permitted slavery in new U.S. territories.

Whatever a Man Could Desire...

> The first white man we knew was a Frenchman ... He smoked his pipe with us, sang and danced with us ... but he wanted to buy no land. The [Englishman] came next ... but never asked us to sell our country to him! Next came the [American] and no sooner had he seen a small portion of our country than he wished us to sell it all to him.
>
> — *Winnebago chief Little Elk*

The earliest Native inhabitants of what we now call Wisconsin probably arrived in the region around eleven thousand years ago after migrating across the North American continent on foot. They used stone points to hunt caribou and mastodon.

Over the next few thousand years, as the climate warmed, Native people began gathering edible fruits, nuts, and wild rice and began using copper, which they found around Lake Superior. In the early 1600s, when the first Europeans arrived, many Native tribes lived in the area that is now Wisconsin. Most of them spoke Algonquian.

Early Settlement

> *I liked noe country as I have that wherein we wintered Washington Island, Wisconsin; for whatever a man could desire was to be had in great plenty; viz. Staggs, fishes in abundance, and all sort of meat, corne enough.*
>
> — Explorer Pierre Esprit Radisson

In early 1634 Samuel de Champlain (the leader of the French colony of New France) sent Jean Nicolet to explore the area that today is Wisconsin and Michigan. Nicolet had come to New France at the age of twenty and had lived with a Native tribe on Allumette Island in the Ottawa River to learn Algonquian language and culture.

Nicolet canoed along the Lake Michigan shore of Michigan's Upper Peninsula. He was seeking a water route to the Pacific Ocean, but the waters took him only as far west as Green Bay, Wisconsin.

Native Americans of Wisconsin

Brotherton
Fox
Huron
Illinois
Kickapoo
Mascouten
Menominee
Miami
Munsee
Ojibwa (Chippewa)
Oneida
Ottawa
Potawatomi
Santee Sioux
Sauk
Stockbridge Mohican
Winnebago (Ho Chunk)

Around 1660 the Roman Catholic priest René Ménard opened a mission on the Chippewa River with the hope of converting Hurons. When the Hurons moved away, Ménard followed them; he was never heard from again. About five years later Father Claude Allouez established several missions.

Most of the first Europeans to reach Wisconsin wanted to convert the Natives to Christianity or to trade for furs. For a time, only the Ottawa traded with the French. In 1671 Nicolas Perrot went to the Algonquian tribes and persuaded them to be loyal to France and to trade with him; in 1685 he became French governor of the region.

For the next hundred years, Europeans regarded Wisconsin as a source of furs. New Native tribes moved into Wisconsin, including tribes from the Iroquois Confederacy (from eastern Canada, New England, and New York) who moved west to take over new fur territory.

In 1764 Frenchman Augustin Monet de Langlade founded the first permanent European settlement in Wisconsin at Green Bay. He married an Ottawa woman named Domitilde. Their son, Charles Langlade, became a prominent fur trader and was later known as the "father of Wisconsin."

▼ The Wisconsin River.

The French and Indian War (1754–1763)

By 1750 English settlers in the Atlantic colonies were seeking more land to farm. The French had claimed the lands west of the Appalachian Mountains, but the English claimed that their charters gave them the rights to these same lands. This set off the final colonial conflict in North America between Great Britain and France, in 1754. The English called it the French and Indian War because many Native tribes fought on the side of the French. At the end of the war in 1763, the British were victorious and acquired Wisconsin.

The Revolutionary War didn't affect Wisconsin much — few traders in Wisconsin even knew about it. When the war was over, the area became part of the United States in 1783. However, British fur traders still controlled the region until 1816, when forts were established at Green Bay and Prairie, opening the region for settlers.

Territory and Statehood

I ordered my squadron to advance in front, and fortunately met with a good position, a natural elevation

▼ A map of Prairie du Chien, circa 1870. Prairie du Chien was the site on which the Treaty of Prairie du Chien was signed in 1825. The treaty robbed Native Americans of the right to their land.

of ground which covered my men who were ordered to squat down, the Enemy raised the Yell and Galloped up within thirty yards of us, we fired on them and killed one and wounded one or two others, when they retreated.
— Henry Dodge, July 22, 1832

The new U.S. settlers were more interested in settling the region and farming it than in hunting for furs, since by the early 1800s there were few fur animals left in Wisconsin. They cleared forests for farms and built houses, roads, and towns.

In 1825 several tribes signed the Treaty of Prairie du Chien (Prairie of the Dog) with the U.S. government. They agreed to establish boundaries to their land. They did not realize that this would eventually cause them to lose their land.

Lead was discovered in the southwest; miners moved to Wisconsin to make their fortunes. The surface mines ran out after a few years, but miners from England came who knew how to mine deep in the earth.

Marquette and Jolliet

The governor of New France wanted to claim as much land as possible for France. He sent men to explore: Louis Jolliet, a fur trader; Father Jacques Marquette, a missionary; and five *voyageurs* ("boatmen"). They canoed into Green Bay in 1634 and down the Fox River. Two Miami men guided the explorers farther than Europeans had ever gone, helping them carry their gear from one river to another. When the explorers entered the Wisconsin River, their Miami guides fled home, afraid of running into the Winnebagos who lived there. Marquette and Jolliet traveled down the Wisconsin River for seven days until they reached the Mississippi River. They went downstream; when they became afraid of running into Spanish explorers, they turned around.

Henry Dodge was a prominent lead miner. He and his followers moved onto Winnebago land and refused to move. The government forced the Winnebago to accept new treaties in 1829, and the Winnebago lost their rights to the rich lead region.

In 1832 Black Hawk (a warrior of the Sauk and Fox tribe) gathered about one thousand Native men, women, and children and marched into Illinois, demanding to be allowed to hunt and grow corn on their ancestral lands. When they failed, they started walking back — but they ran into a militia that ignored their white flag and attacked them. The fighting took weeks; at the end, all but between 100 to 150 of the Native Americans had been killed.

We were proceeding to the Ouisconsin, with our women and children. We arrived and had commenced crossing them to an island, when we discovered a large body of the enemy coming towards us. We were now compelled to fight, or sacrifice our wives and children to the fury of the whites!
— Black Hawk, describing the same battle that Henry Dodge described, above, 1832

The Road to Statehood
In 1787, Wisconsin became part of the Northwest Territory, which also included all or parts of present day Indiana,

◀ Randy Hughes of Rock County carved a 10-acre (4-hectare) maze in his cornfield in celebration of Wisconsin's 150th anniversary as a state.

Illinois, Ohio, Minnesota, and Michigan. Wisconsin became known as Wisconsin Territory in 1836. The first territorial legislature met in the town of Belmont; Dodge was named territorial governor. Nine years later, Wisconsin had the sixty thousand residents necessary for statehood. In 1848 it became the thirtieth state. That same year, Madison became the state capital and home of the University of Wisconsin.

The Civil War and Beyond

Wisconsin had only been a state for a few years when the Civil War began in 1861, but Wisconsinites threw themselves into the fight on the Union side. By the end of the Civil War in 1865, more than 90,000 Wisconsin men had served, including 165 who served in African-American regiments. Wisconsin soldiers served in fifty-two regiments of infantry and four of cavalry, in batteries and regiments of heavy and light artillery, three brigade bands, and one company of sharpshooters.

Immigration to Wisconsin from northern Europe had begun before the Civil War, and many more immigrants came to the state after 1865. By 1880 most of the arable land was being farmed. Not all Wisconsinites were happy about the influx of foreigners, and in 1889 the state legislature passed a law requiring all public school classes to be taught in English. German and Scandinavian workers tried to form unions to empower workers. In 1886 riots broke out among men who were seeking an eight-hour workday. Militias were called out to guard the factories, and one group of soldiers fired into a crowd, killing four men and a child.

The Twentieth Century

When World War I began in 1914, Germany became an enemy of the United States. Many Wisconsinites of German ancestry changed their names to show that they were loyal U.S. citizens.

Soon after the war ended, the Eighteenth Amendment (called Prohibition) made it illegal to sell alcoholic beverages in the United States. Germans in the United States were known for making beer. Some people think that if the United States hadn't fought against Germany in World War I, Prohibition would not have been approved.

The Colors

It was in those days when we were boys or young men that we first began to understand what those flags, what our beautiful national emblem, means. It was in those early days in our experience in the war that we learned to love the stars and stripes, all of the stars, all of the stripes — everything about the dear old flag of our regiment; our flag, wherever it might be.

— *Jerome Watrous of the 6th Wisconsin Civil War regiment, upon the dedication of the Grand Army of the Republic Memorial Hall at the state capitol, June 14, 1918*

In Wisconsin thousands of people who worked in breweries and saloons became unemployed. Many U.S. citizens resented the new law, and in 1933 Prohibition was repealed.

The Great Depression caused more than half of Wisconsin's residents to become unemployed. In 1932 the state passed the nation's first unemployment insurance law. It required that companies set aside money so that they could provide an employee's salary for a while if that person was laid off from work. Today the whole country has unemployment laws such as these.

Wisconsin's progressive spirit didn't start, or end, there, however. In the early 1900s several cities throughout the United States experimented with socialism in local government. Milwaukee went further than any of them. Between 1910 and 1960 there were only twelve years when the city did not have a socialist mayor. Emil Seidel was the first, serving from 1910 to 1912. In 1917 socialist city attorney and foe of government corruption Daniel Webster Hoan was elected. Hoan stayed in office twenty-four years. During his long tenure Hoan battled corruption in city

▼ In October of 1919 Federal Judge Kenesaw Mountain Landis ordered Wisconsin beer to be dumped into Lake Michigan at Chicago, Illinois, due to the federal prohibition laws.

offices and established the city's first public housing development. Like other socialist mayors, Hoan favored municipal ownership of public utilities rather than their management by private companies. While he was mayor, public lighting, water treatment, and sewage disposal all came under the control of the city.

In 1941 Hoan was defeated for reelection, and a Democrat came into power. Seven years later, however, a socialist was back in the mayor's office as Frank Zeider began the first of his twelve years as mayor of Milwaukee.

World War II was a boost to the Wisconsin economy. Once again, Germany was an enemy. When it became clear that the United States would enter the war, the German Americans of Milwaukee held anti-Nazi rallies to demonstrate their loyalty.

More than three hundred thousand Wisconsinites served in the armed forces during World War II. Because Wisconsin was already a major producer of machinery, it was easy for the state to produce machines for war.

Wisconsin Today

Today Wisconsin is a state with great diversity. It is known for its dairy farming, its football teams, its Native reservations (the Menominee are known nationwide for managing their forests in an environmentally friendly way), and for its Wisconsin Works program, the goal of which is to get people off welfare and into the workforce. In 1997 the U.S. government instituted a similar program for the whole country.

McCarthyism

After World War II many Americans feared the growing power of the Soviet Union, which was a communist nation. Wisconsin Senator Joseph R. McCarthy preyed on those fears by accusing U.S. citizens of being communists. He had no real facts, but people believed him, and the lives and careers of some of the accused were ruined. In 1954 he began attacking the U.S. army's leadership. The Senate held hearings to question the people he accused, and millions of U.S. citizens watched him bully people on television and began to realize he had no evidence for his accusations. Support for his ideas waned. (In 1957 he died.) Today the word "McCarthyism" refers to unfair tactics and reckless accusations.

◀ Holstein cows stand in a snowy paddock outside a barn. The classic black-and-white splotched Holsteins are renowned dairy cows.

Communities Coming Together

> When I landed in Madison twelve years ago last spring and first beheld its beautiful lakes and gorgeous scenery, its splendid residences and magnificent educational advantages, I wondered why the streets were not up with the rest of the things . . . I could not realize why the mode of travel at that time was by means of dry-goods boxes on wheels drawn by little Santa Fe Jacks, whose "ye haws" sounded like the sawing of gourds.
>
> — *B. B. Clarke's musings on immigrating to Wisconsin, 1902*

Most of Wisconsin's population is of northern European ancestry. In the 1800s Wisconsin attracted immigrants from all over Europe, but especially from Germany and Scandinavia. In the 1850s 10 percent of all German immigrants who came to the United States settled in Wisconsin.

Pamphlets and books praising Wisconsin were published in Germany and Denmark in the late 1800s, and Racine County soon had more Danes living in it than anywhere else in the United States. South of Milwaukee, meatpacker Patrick Cudahy built a whole community to house the thousands of Polish workers he recruited.

Age Distribution in Wisconsin
(approximate)

0–4	342,340
5–19 years	1,189,753
20–24 years	357,292
25–44 years	1,581,690
45–64 years	1,190,047
65 and over	702,553

Patterns of Immigration

The total number of people who immigrated to Wisconsin in 1998 was 3,724. Of that number, the largest immigrant groups were from Mexico (18%), India (8%), and China (6%).

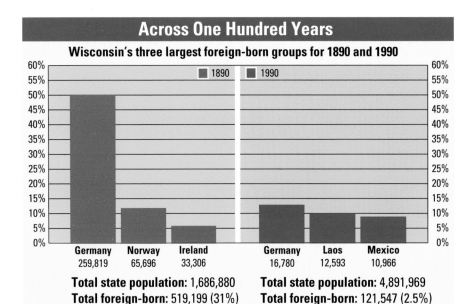

Across One Hundred Years
Wisconsin's three largest foreign-born groups for 1890 and 1990

■ 1890   ■ 1990

Germany	Norway	Ireland	Germany	Laos	Mexico
259,819	65,696	33,306	16,780	12,593	10,966

Total state population: 1,686,880
Total foreign-born: 519,199 (31%)

Total state population: 4,891,969
Total foreign-born: 121,547 (2.5%)

In the late nineteenth and early twentieth centuries, most of Wisconsin's immigrants still came from Germany and the Scandinavian nations. Today Wisconsin is also home to Asian-American and Latino communities. For instance, there is a large and active Hmong population in Wisconsin today. The Hmong are from Laos.

▲ The University of Wisconsin at Madison.

Heritage and Background, Wisconsin — Year 2000

▶ Here's a look at the racial backgrounds of Wisconsinites today. Wisconsin ranks thirtieth in the country with regard to African Americans as a percentage of the population.

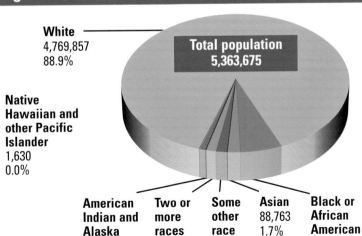

Total population 5,363,675

White
4,769,857
88.9%

Native Hawaiian and other Pacific Islander
1,630
0.0%

American Indian and Alaska Native
47,228
0.9%

Two or more races
66,895
1.2%

Some other race
84,842
1.6%

Asian
88,763
1.7%

Black or African American
304,460
5.7%

Note: About 3.6 percent (192,921) of the population identify themselves as **Hispanic** or **Latino,** a cultural designation that crosses racial lines. Hispanics and Latinos are counted in this category and the racial category of their choice.

Most of the ethnic groups in Wisconsin tend to live in particular areas. Today German Americans live throughout Wisconsin, but there are more of them in the east and in Milwaukee than anywhere else in the state. Polish Americans mostly live in Milwaukee and Stevens Point. Norwegian Americans tend to live in the west and south, and Swedish Americans in the north and northwest. African Americans and Latinos live primarily in the southeastern lakeshore cities of Milwaukee, Racine, and Kenosha. More than four-fifths of Wisconsin's African Americans

Educational Levels of Wisconsin Workers	
Less than 9th grade	294,862
9th to 12th grade, no diploma	367,210
High school graduate, including equivalency	1,147,697
Some college, no degree	735,427
Associate degree	392,869
Bachelor's degree	375,603
Graduate or professional degree	173,367

▼ The riverfront in Milwaukee, Wisconsin's largest city.

live in metropolitan Milwaukee, where they make up nearly one-third of the population.

The Native American population is concentrated largely in the city of Milwaukee and in Menominee County. The Ojibwa, Menominee, Ho-Chunk (formerly Winnebago), and Potawatomi still live in Wisconsin; so do four other tribes that migrated from the east in the 1820s (Stockbridge Mohican, Munsee, Brotherton, and Oneida).

▲ In this undated historical photograph, a group of Ojibwas pose in front of bark dwellings at Odama.

From the Great Depression of the 1930s to the late 1960s, northern Wisconsin generally lost population, but since that time the downward trend has reversed. Still, most Wisconsinites live in the southeast. The soil and climate there are good for farming, which is why that area was settled first.

Wisconsin is speckled with towns of fewer than one thousand people, but its major cities are in the southeast. Milwaukee, combined with its satellite cities, is a major manufacturing center and port. Madison, located between Lakes Mendota and Monona, is where the University of Wisconsin is based. Racine and Kenosha, on Lake Michigan south of Milwaukee, are small ports and produce tractors and metal goods.

Religion

Wisconsin's immigrants brought diverse religious affiliations to the state. The Norwegians who immigrated there were mostly Lutheran, the Germans were both Lutheran and Roman Catholic, the Poles were Roman Catholic, and many of the others were non-Lutheran Protestant. Today about 90 percent of Wisconsin residents identify themselves as Christian.

Nearly 40 percent of Wisconsin's Christian population is Catholic, while nearly 20 percent is Lutheran. The remainder is divided among other Christian denominations such as Episcopalian, Methodist, and Presbyterian. Wisconsinites who do not belong to Christian churches include the 0.7 percent who are Jewish, 0.3 percent who are Buddhist, and 0.2 percent who are Muslim.

From Forests to Fields

> Oh, that glorious Wisconsin wilderness! Everything new and pure . . . flowers, animals, the winds and the streams and the sparkling lake.
> — *John Muir*

W isconsin's landscape is rich and varied. The state is home to many rivers and lakes; it is both a patchwork of farms and a home to industrial cities such as Milwaukee, Green Bay, Racine, Kenosha, Beloit, Oshkosh, and Janesville.

Most of Wisconsin's landscape was shaped by the glaciers of the last ice age, which left boulders, round ponds called kettles, and piles of debris called moraines all over the state. In the south and central west of the state is a patch of land the glacier missed; it is called the Driftless Area.

Climate

Wisconsin has long, cold winters and short, warm summers. Average temperatures in January range from 10° Fahrenheit (-12° Celsius) in the north to 22°F (-6°C) in the southeast; in July, from 66°F (19°C) in the north to 72°F (22°C) in the southeast. The Great Lakes mellow temperatures along their coasts. Annual rainfall averages about 30 inches (76 centimeters), most of it falling between May and October. Snowfall varies from about 30 inches (76 centimeters) in the south at Beloit to over 100 inches (254 cm) in northern Iron

High Point

Timms Hill
1,951 feet (595 m)
above sea level

▼ *From left to right:* **Locks on the Mississippi River at Alma; the woods in winter; a view of Milwaukee from Lake Michigan; a snowshoe hare; historic Stonefield Village in Cassville; a loon.**

County. Streams and lakes are usually frozen from December to mid-April.

Neighbors

To the north Wisconsin is bordered by the western portion of Lake Superior and the Upper Peninsula of Michigan. Minnesota and Iowa lie to the west and southwest. Illinois lies to the south and Lake Michigan to the east. The state's land area is 54,310 square miles (140,663 sq km).

The northern part of the state, called the Northern Highland, is made of granite bedrock. It contains the state's highest point, Timms Hill. Nearby is the Lake Superior Lowland, a narrow plain that slopes down to a central sandstone plain in the middle of the state.

The southwest is etched by streams into ridges and valleys. In the southeast three broad limestone ridges run north to south, separating shallow lowlands.

The lowest elevation in the state is along the shore of Lake Michigan at 581 feet (177 m) above sea level. Where the glaciers once were are now rolling hills dotted with marshes and lakes and often with boulders.

Lakes and Rivers

The state's major river is the Wisconsin, 430 miles (692 km) long. It begins on the Michigan border and flows south, toward Madison. It goes around the Baraboo Range before turning west to enter the Mississippi River near Prairie du Chien. Other rivers include the Chippewa, St. Croix, Wolf, Namekagon, Brule, Menominee, and Pike.

All of these are in northern Wisconsin. This region, along with neighbor Minnesota, has one of the largest concentrations of lakes in the world. Wisconsin has nearly fifteen thousand lakes of more than 20 acres (8 ha) — that's more than 1,500 square miles (3,885 sq km) of lakes! The

Average January temperature
Madison: 16°F (-9°C)
Superior: 10°F (-12°C)

Average July temperature
Madison: 71°F (22°C)
Superior: 66°F (19°C)

Average yearly rainfall
Madison:
 30 inches (76 cm)
Superior:
 29.6 inches (75 cm)

Average yearly snowfall
Madison:
 39 inches (99 cm)
Superior:
 76.9 inches (195 cm)

Major Rivers

Mississippi River
2,350 miles
 (3,780 km) long
231 miles (372 km)
 along the Wisconsin
 border

Wisconsin River
430 miles (692 km)

Chippewa River
200 miles (320 km)

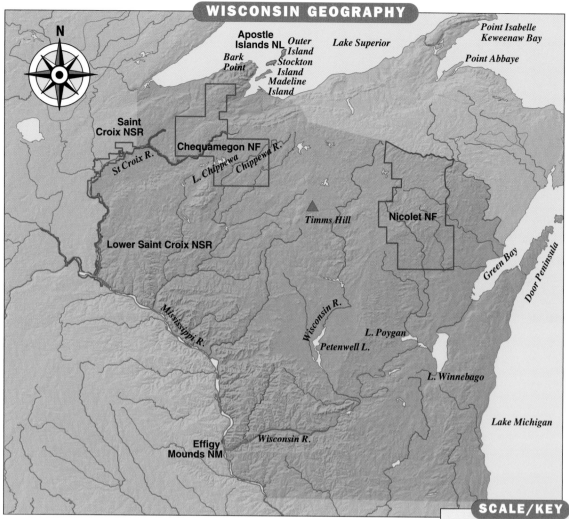

0	50 Miles
0	50 Kilometers

NL National Lakeshore

NF National Forest

NSR National Scenic River

▲ Highest Point

Mountains

largest is Lake Winnebago (215 square miles, 557 sq km) in the Fox River Valley.

Included in Wisconsin's boundary waters are 7,387 square miles (19,132 sq km) of Lake Michigan and 2,675 square miles (6,928 sq km) of Lake Superior. Lake Superior is the largest freshwater lake in the world and is famous for its storms, which have sunk many ships over the centuries.

Wildlife

Forests once covered about 85 percent of the state; the rest was prairies and wetlands. Most of the forests were cleared for lumber and agriculture, but today nearly 45 percent of Wisconsin is again forested.

Most of Wisconsin's trees are second-growth hardwoods (maple, birch, oak, aspen, elm, basswood, and ash) and evergreens (white, red, and jack pine, hemlock, balsam fir, black spruce, white cedar, and tamarack).

Common animals in Wisconsin include white-tailed deer, foxes, cottontail rabbits, skunks, woodchucks, squirrels, chipmunks, and gophers. Black bears, coyotes, wolves, porcupines, beavers, otters, snowshoe hares, and eagles live in the north. On the lakes and rivers live many waterbirds, including geese, ducks, and loons; fish include panfish, trout, bass, walleye, northern pike and sturgeon.

Environment

Wisconsin has been home to some of the nation's foremost environmentalists. One was Aldo Leopold, a forester with the U.S. Forest Service who established a wildlife management program at the University of Wisconsin. Another was John Muir, who emigrated from Scotland to Marquette County in 1849 at the age of eleven. Muir founded the Sierra Club, one of the most influential environmental protection organizations in the world.

As a result of Wisconsin's history of mining and manufacturing, not all of its environment is pristine. The state currently offers advisories on which fish are safe to eat (some of the state's waters are contaminated with mercury and polychlorinated biphenyls, or PCBs), and private industry and the Department of Natural Resources continue to seek ways to work together to diminish polution.

Largest Lakes

Lake Winnebago
137,708 acres
(55,730 ha)
21 feet (6 m) maximum depth

Petenwell Lake
23,040 acres
(8,324 ha)
44 feet (13 m) maximum depth

Lake Chippewa
15,300 acres (619 ha)
92 feet (28 m) maximum depth

Lake Poygan
14,102 acres (5,207 ha)
11 feet (3 m) maximum depth

▼ Autumn scenery in Minocqua, northern Wisconsin.

From Furs to Dairy Farms

> Remember when our good friends down in Illinois mocked our troubled economy? They even went so far as to put up a billboard on the border saying, 'When the last business leaves Wisconsin, please turn out the lights.' Well my friends, the lights are on in Wisconsin and burning brighter than ever.
>
> — *Governor Scott McCallum, January 2001*

Wisconsin's first economy was fur-based; Native Americans sold animal pelts to Europeans, and then settlers trapped animals themselves. When the pelts ran out, valuable mineral deposits were discovered in the state, and mining became the mainstay of Wisconsin's economy. The state's nickname, "The Badger State," comes from its history of mining — miners tunnel underground as do badgers.

Southeast Wisconsin is an industrial belt that extends along Lake Michigan from the Chicago area to Milwaukee, the state's largest city. It is the primary factor in making Wisconsin one of the top fifteen states in industrial output. Wisconsin is a leader in the manufacturing of machinery and produces more paper than any other state.

Dairy farms in the southern two-thirds of the state make Wisconsin second only to California as the nation's leader in producing milk and milk-products. The state also produces more than one-quarter of the nation's cheese. In the sparsely settled northern part of the state, forests and lakes host tourist and recreational activities.

Wisconsin is known for having a strong labor policy that tries to create jobs and provide safety nets for those who are unemployed.

Mining

Early mining in Wisconsin began in the southwestern part of the state at Mineral Point, founded in 1827 when

Top Employers
(of workers age sixteen and over; totals add up to more than 100% as some residents hold two or more jobs)

Services	29.9%
Manufacturing	24.5%
Wholesale and retail trade	21.1%
Government workers	12.9%
Finance, insurance, and real estate	5.8%
Construction	4.9%
Agriculture, forestry, and fisheries	4.5%
Transportation	3.7%
Communications and other public utilities	1.9%
Mining	1.0%

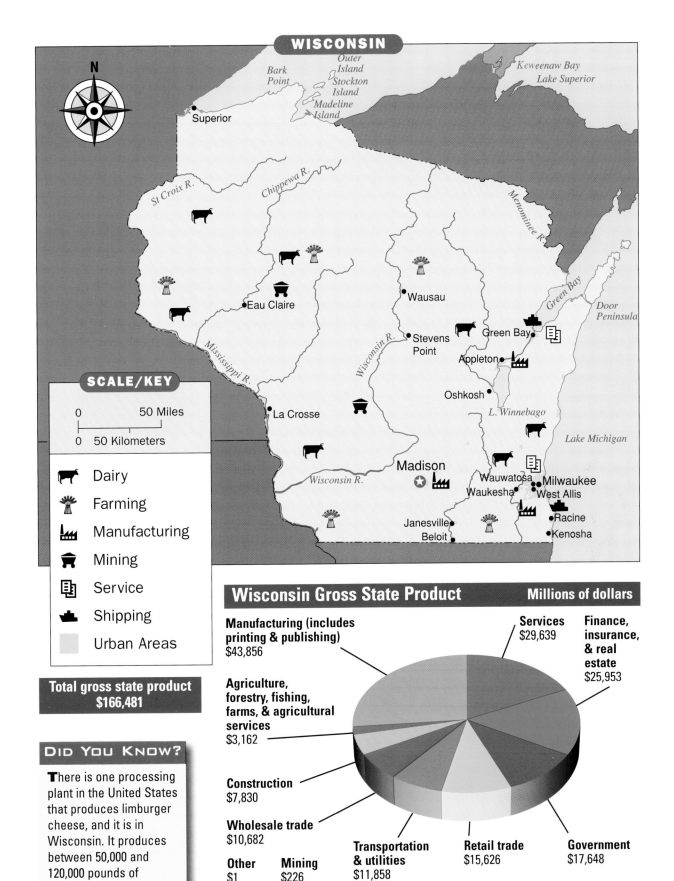

WISCONSIN

N

Bark Point
Outer Island
Stockton Island
Madeline Island
Keweenaw Bay
Lake Superior

Superior

St Croix R.

Chippewa R.

Menominee R.

Green Bay

Door Peninsula

Eau Claire

Wausau

Stevens Point

Green Bay

Appleton

Mississippi R.

Wisconsin R.

Oshkosh

L. Winnebago

Lake Michigan

SCALE/KEY

0	50 Miles
0	50 Kilometers

La Crosse

Madison

Wisconsin R.

Wauwatosa
Waukesha

Milwaukee
West Allis

🐄 Dairy

🌾 Farming

🏭 Manufacturing

⛏ Mining

🗃 Service

🚢 Shipping

Urban Areas

Janesville
Beloit

Racine

Kenosha

Total gross state product
$166,481

Wisconsin Gross State Product — Millions of dollars

Manufacturing (includes printing & publishing)
$43,856

Agriculture, forestry, fishing, farms, & agricultural services
$3,162

Construction
$7,830

Wholesale trade
$10,682

Other
$1

Mining
$226

Transportation & utilities
$11,858

Retail trade
$15,626

Government
$17,648

Services
$29,639

Finance, insurance, & real estate
$25,953

deposits of lead ore were found there. Both bullets and paint were made from lead in those days, so it was a valuable resource. When lead prices fell and food prices rose, farmers started settling in southwestern Wisconsin.

In the mid 1970s the Exxon Corporation found zinc sulfide and copper deposits in Forest County next to the Sokaogon Chippewa Indian Community and the headwaters of the Wolf River. Today the Nicolet Mineral Company wants to open a huge mine, with a shaft about 2,200 feet (670 m) deep. It would employ a lot of people, but many oppose its creation because they fear it would create pollution.

▼ Wisconsin produces more than 18 million pounds (8,164,800 kilograms) of cheese annually.

Farming

Throughout most of the nineteenth century, New York was the top U.S. source of cheese. That changed when Wisconsin dairy farmers planted an English grass that made their cows produce better milk. In 1871, when refrigerated railroad cars became available, Wisconsin cheese was able to be transported to the east, and its fame began to grow. Since 1920 Wisconsin has ranked at or near the top in the country in dairy products. Wisconsin residents (and fans of the state's professional football team, the Green Bay Packers) are known as "Cheeseheads."

Meatpacking is another Wisconsin enterprise. Oscar Mayer moved his sausage business from Chicago to Madison, and today it is one of the largest meat product companies in the world.

Wisconsin is also known for its sweet corn, green beans, peas, and cranberries.

◄ In 1903 two young men from Milwaukee, William Harley and Arthur Davidson, worked in a shack to build a racing motorcycle. Ninety years later, more than one hundred thousand participated in their anniversary parade, and by the year 2000, the Harley-Davidson company was earning $2.9 billion a year.

Forests and Fishing

In the 1870s commercial lumbering reached Wisconsin's northern forests. Timber exploitation continued for about forty years, leaving a devastated countryside that has only begun to recover in the last fifty years.

Today most of Wisconsin's logged timber — mostly aspen and pine — is turned into pulpwood. This is why Wisconsin produces more paper than any other state. Some hardwoods, such as red oak, aspen, and elm, are cut for use in building and manufacturing.

Commercial fishing also contributes to the Wisconsin economy. From the 1940s to 1960s, the sea lamprey (introduced accidentally into the Great Lakes) destroyed much of the region's fish stock, making fishing almost impossible. Since then, people have restocked lake trout, whitefish, lake herring, and other fish, which can now be fished commercially. Sport fishing is also popular, thanks to the introduction of some Pacific Northwest fish into the area.

Today there is some conflict between commercial and sport fishers and Native peoples over fishing rights. In some places Native American, commercial, and sport fishers are all limited to a certain quantity of fish each year. In other places, depending on local laws, treaties, and reservation boundaries, Native Americans are permitted to fish as much as they please, while other fishers must abide by quotas.

▲ *Top:* A meatpacking plant. *Above:* Four generations of Usingers have been producing hot dogs and sausages at the family's company in Milwaukee. The quality of their hot dogs led the U.S. Olympic Committee to choose Usingers as the official supplier to the 2002 Winter Olympics.

Major Airports		
Airport	Location	Passengers per year (2000)
General Mitchell International	Milwaukee	6,076,628
Austin Straubel International	Green Bay	720,000
Dane County Regional Airport	Madison	668,731

Progressive Politics

Many cities are named after great Americans, but none greater than Madison. The author of the Constitution was a great believer in government, in the proper role of government, in limited government. He also understood, perhaps better than anyone else of his time or any time since, the delicate balance between state and federal governments. How fortunate for the people of Wisconsin to have a state capital named Madison.

— *Harold Furchtgott-Roth, head of the Federal Communications Commission, 2000*

Wisconsin Government Today

Like the national government, Wisconsin's government is made up of three branches: executive, legislative, and judicial.

The executive branch is headed by the governor and lieutenant governor; other officials in that branch include the secretary of state, state treasurer, and attorney general.

The Wisconsin Legislature is *bicameral*, or divided into two houses, the Assembly and the Senate. Representatives elected to the Assembly serve two-year terms; senators serve four-year terms. There are ninety-nine Assembly members and thirty-three senators.

The judicial branch is headed by the state supreme court, which is made up of seven justices who serve for ten years each. This branch also includes the state's court of appeals, which divides the state into four districts for hearing cases that are appealed from lower courts, and about two hundred local or regional courts.

Today the state's capitol is in Madison, a city named after President James Madison and built on an isthmus (a land bridge between two lakes). In 1904 the capitol building caught fire, and most of it burned; it was thirteen

DID YOU KNOW?

On July 29, 1915, the Wisconsin State Legislature approved the purchase of an electric vote-tallier. Two years later, on January 11, the machine was installed making the state the first to use such a device, which saved both time and money. The roll call of legislators could be made in eleven seconds, resulting in savings of 99 percent.

DID YOU KNOW?

Tommy Thompson, Republican governor of Wisconsin from 1987 to 2001, was appointed United States Secretary of Health and Human Services in 2001. While governor, he established Wisconsin Works, a welfare-reform program that served as a model for other states.

Elected Posts in the Executive Branch		
Office	Length of Term	Term Limits
Governor	4 years	None
Lieutenant Governor	4 years	None
Secretary of State	4 years	None
Attorney General	4 years	None
Treasurer and Receiver General	4 years	None
State Auditor	4 years	None

▼ The state capitol in Madison was built between 1906 and 1917.

years before a new one was finished. The capitol building has four identical entrances but no official front door; its dome stands almost 300 feet (91 m) high.

Since 1848, when Wisconsin became a state, its constitution has been amended 132 times but has never been rewritten.

Progressive Ideas

I made it a policy, in order to bring all the reserves of knowledge and inspiration of the university more to the service of the people, to appoint experts from the university wherever possible upon the important boards of the state — the civil service commission, the railroad commission and so on — a relationship which the university has always encouraged and by which the state has greatly profited.

— Robert La Follette, 1911

Two big political movements, the Wisconsin Idea and the Progressive movement, arose from Wisconsin. Both came into being in the early twentieth century, thanks to Wisconsin's representatives in Washington, D.C. A third movement may also have started in Wisconsin — the Republican Party.

In 1854 the U.S. Congress passed a law that allowed slavery to spread into the new Kansas Territory. Many antislavery Northerners were angry, and opponents of the new law met to decide what to do. In Ripon, Wisconsin, a group met on February 28, 1854; the men there decided to start a new political party to fight the spread of slavery. They called themselves Republicans. A similar meeting also took place in Michigan around the same time, so the two states disagree about who actually founded the Republican Party.

By the end of the nineteenth century, most of Wisconsin's wealth and power was controlled by railroad and timber barons. Robert M. "Fighting Bob" La Follette wanted to make government "a servant, not a ruler, of people." He campaigned around the state, giving speeches to farmers and laborers who were thrilled to have a politician pay attention to them and their needs.

La Follette served as Wisconsin's governor and later as a senator. He called himself a Progressive Republican to show that he was different from the rest of the Republican Party. He championed ideas such as protecting state forests, fixing railway rates so that they would not vary depending on how friendly a shipper was with the railway owners, and paying government employees based on their merit, not their social standing. La Follette is credited with helping to start the Progressive movement.

Journalist Lincoln Steffens, who knew La Follette, wrote that he was "a fighter — for peace; he battered his fist so terribly in one great speech for peace during the World War that he had to be treated and then carried it in bandages for weeks."

▲ Robert La Follette, political reformer and founder of Wisconsin's Progressive Party.

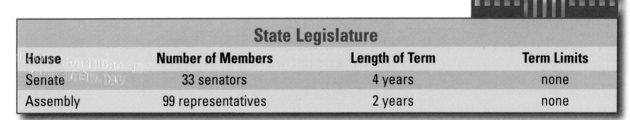

State Legislature			
House	Number of Members	Length of Term	Term Limits
Senate	33 senators	4 years	none
Assembly	99 representatives	2 years	none

La Follette's legacy continued after his death. His son Robert Jr. represented Wisconsin in Congress from 1925 to 1947; his other son Philip served three terms as governor, from 1931 to 1933 and 1935 to 1939 (until the 1970s, Wisconsin governors served two-year terms).

Although the Progressive movement was a strong political force in the state, it was part of the state Republican Party until 1934, when it separated to become the Wisconsin Progressive Party. In 1946 it rejoined the Republicans, but many adherents went instead to the Democratic Party.

Although the Republican Party got its start in Wisconsin, voter loyalties have changed, and it has not always dominated local or state politics. Since the late 1950s, five of the last nine Wisconsin governors have been Democrats, and the state voted Democratic in the presidential elections of 1992, 1996, and 2000. Democrats often held a majority in the legislature at the end of the twentieth century. Republican governor Tommy Thompson, however, was reelected three times after his first term in 1987 before he became U.S. Secretary of Health and Human Services in 2001.

▲ The Wisconsin State Legislature in session.

The Wisconsin Idea

Thanks to the movement for genuinely democratic popular government which Senator La Follette led to overwhelming victory in Wisconsin, that state has become literally a laboratory for wise experimental legislation aiming to secure the social and political betterment of the people as a whole.
— Theodore Roosevelt, 1912

One outgrowth of the Progressive movement was the Wisconsin Idea. Its theme was, "The boundaries of the university campus are the boundaries of the state," and it was an effort to bring together the resources of state government, the state university system, and citizens' groups to solve social, political, and economic problems.

Another part of the Wisconsin Idea involved establishing an income tax. The government used that income tax to improve the quality of life in Wisconsin. The tax money paid for improvements such as roads and better schools.

Art in the Heartland

> There is only one way to succeed in anything, and that is to give it everything.
> — *Green Bay Packers coach Vince Lombardi*

Today Wisconsin is settled by people of almost every ethnicity and heritage imaginable. In its early years the state was settled by a small number of ethnic groups, who still give the state much of its cultural flavor.

Many ethnic groups settled in enclaves, and each brought its own art, music, and folk culture to Wisconsin. The state is known for its cultural festivals and fairs, including Asian, Polish, African, Irish, Italian, German, Arabian, and Mexican festivals in Milwaukee throughout the summer. Native American ceremonial gatherings take place in September.

Wisconsin's Holiday Folk Fair is the oldest and largest multiethnic festival in the country. One of the state's largest celebrations is Summerfest, which is among the world's biggest music festivals. Summerfest happens in Milwaukee, but there's fun in the countryside, too; the whole state is home to county fairs.

Many Wisconsinites have become nationally known in the arts. The list includes writers John Muir, Thornton Wilder, and Edna Ferber; actors Alfred Lunt and Lynn Fontaine; and architect Frank Lloyd Wright.

The University of Wisconsin was the first university in the country to sponsor an artist in residence, the painter John Steuart Curry (1936). It supports the Fine Arts Quartet in Milwaukee and the Pro Arte String Quartet in Madison, groups that have an excellent international reputation. In the summer it operates music clinics for high school students from throughout the country.

In 1957 the University of Wisconsin Extension helped create the Wisconsin Arts Foundation and Council, which in

DID YOU KNOW?

While Wisconsinites claim that the hamburger sandwich was invented at the Seymour Fair, now known as the Outagamie County Fair, the sandwich's history is somewhat more murky. Connecticut, Kansas, and Missouri also lay claim to the invention. This Wisconsin fair can, however, lay claim to having grilled the largest hamburger in the world, in 1989. It weighed 5,520 pounds (2,504 kg).

1970 became an official state agency. In 1973 it became the Wisconsin Arts Board; its goal is to give help to groups and individuals in the arts.

Milwaukee is a major arts center. One of its most famous buildings is the nineteenth-century Pabst Theater, which was recently restored. Milwaukee is also home to the Marcus Center for the

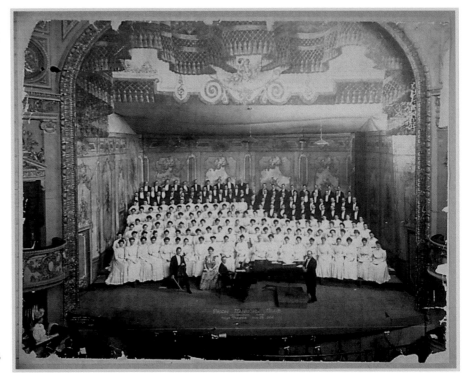

Performing Arts, where many groups perform, including the Milwaukee Symphony Orchestra, the Florentine Opera (the state's oldest performing arts organization), the Bel Canto Chorus, and the Milwaukee Ballet. The Milwaukee Art Museum (more than a hundred years old) has a large collection of contemporary art and works by European and American masters. The Golda Meir Library on the University of Wisconsin–Milwaukee campus contains the

▲ The Arion Musical Club performs at the Pabst Theater in Milwaukee on November 26, 1906.

◀ An artist's rendering of the dramatic new wing of the Milwaukee Art Museum, designed by Spanish architect Santiago Calatrava.

near priceless map collection of the American Geographical Society.

Among the state's many museums is the Circus World Museum in Baraboo, which collects and displays artifacts and other materials from circuses around the world.

Education

Public schools were opened in Wisconsin in 1816, when the children of soldiers stationed at Green Bay, Portage, and Prairie du Chien began attending classes.

When the University of Wisconsin was founded in 1848, there was only one public high school in the state! The others were all church-related academies.

In the 1850s some educators decided that children would learn more if they started school earlier with a kind of special, organized play. They created something called kindergarten (German for "garden of children"). The first kindergarten in the nation opened in Watertown in 1856.

▲ Teens participate in the Anoka Halloween Festival.

The oldest institution of higher learning in Wisconsin is Nashotah House, an Episcopal seminary in Nashotah that was founded in 1841. It is still open today. Lawrence University, in Appleton, was coeducational from the moment it opened its doors in 1847; the University of Wisconsin became co-ed during the Civil War, when there were not enough male students to keep it open. The university has campuses in many cities throughout the state. Among

Sport	Team	Home
Baseball	Milwaukee Brewers	Miller Park, Milwaukee
Basketball	Milwaukee Bucks	Bradley Center, Milwaukee
Football	Green Bay Packers	Lambeau Field, Green Bay

Wisconsin's other universities and colleges are Marquette University (Milwaukee; founded 1857), and Beloit (Beloit; 1846), Carroll (Waukesha; 1846), Carthage (Kenosha; 1847), Ripon (Ripon; 1863), and St. Norbert (De Pere; 1898) colleges. The school of architecture on the grounds of Taliesin, the home of Frank Lloyd Wright near Spring Green, is a mecca for both students and experienced architects.

Sports

Wisconsin is home to three big-league professional sports teams — the Green Bay Packers (football), the Milwaukee Brewers (baseball), and the Milwaukee Bucks (basketball).

▼ The Green Bay Packers take on the Chicago Bears.

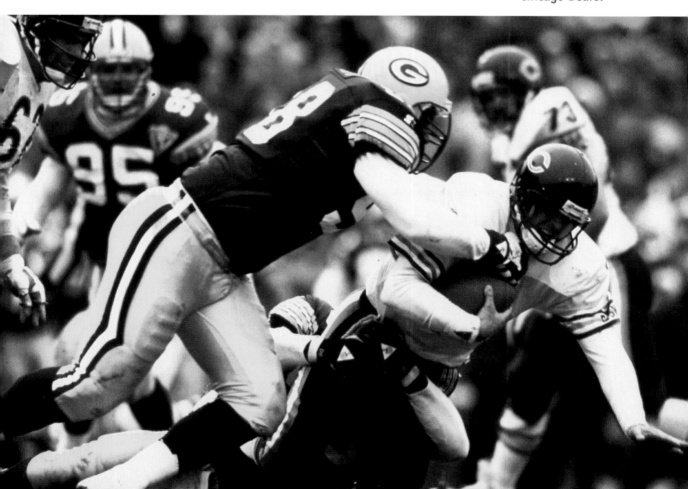

The Packers were organized by Earl Louis "Curly" Lambeau in 1919. The team was sponsored by the Acme Meat Packing Company, which gave it its name. In 1936 shares in the ownership of the team were sold to the citizens of Green Bay. Citizens of the town still own the team.

The Packers won the first two Super Bowl games; they won again in 1997. Devoted fans around the country call themselves "Cheeseheads," and even on the coldest days in December, there is never an empty seat at Lambeau Field. In fact there is a thirty-year waiting list for those who want to purchase season tickets!

Milwaukee's first baseball team was the Braves, who moved from Boston in 1953; within four years they defeated the New York Yankees in the 1957 World Series. In 1966 the team moved to Atlanta; in 1972 the Milwaukee Brewers were founded. In 1982 the team won the American League pennant but fell to the St. Louis Cardinals in the World Series.

In 1968 the Milwaukee Bucks joined the National Basketball Association (NBA). They were champions of the NBA in 1971, led by center Lew Alcindor, who changed his name to Kareem Abdul-Jabbar when he converted to Islam. In 2001 the Bucks advanced to the Eastern Conference finals.

There are also several minor league baseball teams and collegiate teams of various schools, including the Big Ten Conference teams of the University of Wisconsin–Madison.

▲ Milwaukee Brewers' Devon White connects for a grand slam.

Poets, Magicians & More

I'm just a small-town boy from Elroy, Wisconsin . . .
The people of Elroy raised me. Taught me my values.
And instilled in me the importance of putting people first.
— *Tommy G. Thompson, Secretary of Health and Human Services,*
February 2, 2001, Great Hall, Washington, D.C.

Following are only a few of the thousands of people who lived, died, or spent most of their lives in Wisconsin and made extraordinary contributions to the state and the nation.

RINGLING BROTHERS
CIRCUS FOUNDERS

Albert C. (1852–1916),
Otto (1858–1911),
Alfred T. (1861–1919),
Charles (1863–1926), and
John (1866–1936) Ringling.

The sons of August Rüngeling, a German harness maker, Charles, Albert, Otto, Alfred, and John created the Classic and Comic Concert Company in 1882 and took their songs and dances on the road. Soon they added circus acts to their show, and in 1884 they assembled a small circus in their hometown, Baraboo. Then they took the circus to tour the Midwest. They became well known when they bought their first elephant in 1888. In 1890 the Ringling Brothers started loading their circus wagons on railway cars, which allowed them to tour farther. By 1900 the Ringling Brothers were competing with the Barnum & Bailey Circus. They bought the Forepaugh-Sells Circus in 1906, and the Barnum & Bailey Circus in 1907, which made them the biggest circus in the country.

CARRIE CHAPMAN CATT
SUFFRAGIST

BORN: *January 9, 1859, Ripon*
DIED: *March 9, 1947, New Rochelle, NY*

Carrie Chapman Catt, born Carrie Lane, grew up in Ripon, Wisconsin. She graduated from Iowa State College in 1880 and became a high school principal. Two years later, she was appointed superintendent of schools, one of the first women to hold that kind of position. Her first husband, Leo Chapman, an editor, died in 1886, two years after they were married. From then until 1890 she devoted herself to organizing the Iowa Woman Suffrage Association. Her marriage to George W. Catt, an engineer, in 1890, was unusual because they signed a prenuptial agreement that guaranteed her four months each year to work for women's suffrage. She was instrumental in getting women the right to vote.

LAURA INGALLS WILDER

WRITER

BORN: *Feb. 7, 1867, Lake Pepin*
DIED: *Feb. 10, 1957, Mansfield, MO*

The Ingalls family traveled by covered wagon to Minnesota, Iowa, Missouri, Kansas, and Dakota Territory when Laura was a girl. At fifteen she began teaching in rural schools. In 1885 she married Almanzo J. Wilder. Once married, she started writing. She wrote articles for *McCall's Magazine* and *Country Gentleman,* became poultry editor for the *St. Louis Star,* and then spent twelve years as home editor of the *Missouri Ruralist.* Her daughter asked her to write down her childhood experiences; she did, and they were published. In 1932 she published *Little House in the Big Woods,* which was set in Wisconsin. After writing *Farmer Boy* (1933), about Almanzo's childhood, she published *Little House on the Prairie* (1935), about

the time she spent in "Indian Territory" as a girl. Wilder also wrote *On the Banks of Plum Creek* (1937), *By the Shores of Silver Lake* (1939), *The Long Winter* (1940), *Little Town on the Prairie* (1941), and *These Happy Golden Years* (1943).

FRANK LLOYD WRIGHT

ARCHITECT

BORN: *June 8, 1867, Richland Center*
DIED: *April 9, 1959, Phoenix, AZ*

Frank Lloyd Wright (originally named Frank Lincoln Wright) was an architect and writer. Some people consider him the most creative genius of U.S. architecture. He attended the

▲ The Johnson Wax Building in Racine was designed by Frank Lloyd Wright.

University of Wisconsin at Madison from 1885 to 1886 as a special student, but there were no architecture classes, so he studied engineering instead. Wright worked for the dean of engineering to make some money and help support his family, but he did not like the architecture around him and dreamed of a new Midwestern architecture. Other young architects agreed with him; their vision became known as the Prairie School of architecture. By 1900 Prairie School architecture was becoming popular, and Wright, thirty-three years old and mostly self-taught, was at its forefront. The Prairie School featured mass-produced materials and wide-open spaces; it became the basis of twentieth-century residential design in the United States.

HARRY HOUDINI
MAGICIAN

BORN: *March 24, 1874, Budapest, Hungary*
DIED: *Oct. 31, 1926, Detroit, MI*

Harry Houdini's original name was Erik Weisz; he was the son of a rabbi from Hungary who moved to Appleton, Wisconsin. Houdini learned the trapeze at an early age. In 1882 he moved to New York and joined the vaudeville scene there. Starting around 1900, Houdini became famous for his ability to escape from shackles, ropes, and handcuffs and from locked containers such as coffins, giant milk cans, and prison cells. One typical act had him shackled with chains and placed in a box that was locked, tied, and weighted. He would free himself from the box underwater and then return to the boat that had dropped him overboard. In another act he allowed himself to be hung, head down, about 75 feet (23 m) above ground; he would then free himself from a straitjacket in midair.

GOLDA MEIR
STATESWOMAN

BORN: *May 3, 1898, Kiev, Russia*
DIED: *Dec. 8, 1978, Jerusalem, Israel*

In 1906 Goldie Mabovitch's family immigrated to Milwaukee. She attended the Milwaukee Normal School. As a young adult, she became a leader in the Milwaukee Labor Zionist Party. In 1921 she and her husband, Morris Myerson, immigrated to Palestine and joined a kibbutz. She became secretary of the Women's Labour Council there in 1928. After World War II she became head of the Political Department of the Jewish Agency. She made a personal visit to King Abdullah of Jordan to try to convince him not to join the multistate Arab invasion of Israel. In 1959 she changed her name to its Hebrew version. In 1969 Meir became prime minister of Israel. Meir worked hard for a diplomatic peace settlement in the Middle East but was not successful; she stepped down in 1974 and died four years later.

JOHN BARDEEN
PHYSICIST

BORN: *May 23, 1908, Madison*
DIED: *Jan. 30, 1991, Boston, MA*

John Bardeen graduated from the University of Wisconsin at Madison with a doctorate in mathematical physics and, from 1938 to 1941, served as the U.S. Naval Ordnance's principal physicist. It was at Bell Labs, however, that Bardeen first made his mark. He and colleagues William B. Shockley and Walter H. Brattain invented the transistor, which allowed for amazing leaps forward in electronic technology. Transistors control the flow of energy in electronic devices. In 1972 Bardeen was awarded the Nobel Prize in physics, along with colleagues Leon N. Cooper and John R. Schrieffer, for his work in superconductivity. Superconductors allow for the fast, near frictionless movement of electricity.

VINCE LOMBARDI

COACH

BORN: *June 11, 1913, Brooklyn, NY*
DIED: *Sept. 3, 1970, Washington, D.C.*

Vince Lombardi's name has become synonymous with determination to win. "Winning isn't everything," he once said, "It's the only thing." At Fordham University in New York City, Lombardi was part of a group of linemen called the "Seven Blocks of Granite." He was hired to coach the Green Bay Packers in February of 1959. He imposed a very strenuous regimen (which some critics called Spartan or fanatical) on his players, most of whom hadn't won a game in a long time. In nine seasons (1959–1968) as head coach of the Packers, he led the team to five National Football League (NFL) championships and to victory in the first two Super Bowl games.

ORSON WELLES

ACTOR, DIRECTOR, PRODUCER, AND WRITER

BORN: *May 6, 1915, Kenosha*
DIED: *October 10, 1985, Los Angeles, CA*

At age eleven George Orson Welles had already traveled around the world twice, and his adventurous life was just beginning. He began a career on stage in 1931, moved on to

have a career in radio, and there had one of his most famous moments. He and his colleagues adapted works of literature for the radio, and their adaptation of H. G. Wells's *War of the Worlds* (1938) inadvertently convinced listeners that invaders from outer space were attacking New Jersey. From radio he went to Hollywood and created one of the most enduring works in the American cinema — *Citizen Kane* (1941).

WILLIAM H. REHNQUIST

JURIST

BORN: *October 1, 1924, Milwaukee*

The sixteenth chief justice of the Supreme Court, William Hubbs Rehnquist grew up in Milwaukee. After graduating from Stanford University and Stanford Law School, he clerked for Supreme Court Justice Robert H. Jackson, and then he became involved in Republican Party politics. Rehnquist was nominated to the U.S. Supreme Court in 1971 by President Richard Nixon, and he became chief justice in 1986.

◀ Orson Welles.

Wisconsin
History At-A-Glance

1634
French explorer Jean Nicolet enters the area.

Circa 1660
Roman Catholic Priest René Ménard opens a mission along the Chippewa River.

1673
Louis Jolliet and Jacques Marquette reach the Mississippi River.

1685
Nicolas Perrot becomes the French governor for the region.

1754–63
French and Indian War; at the war's end, France cedes to Britain all territories east of the Mississippi.

1764
The first permanent European settlement in Wisconsin is built near Green Bay.

1783
With the end of the Revolutionary War, Britain cedes western territories to the United States.

1825
Several Wisconsin Native American tribes sign the Treaty of Prairie du Chien, which eventually leads to the loss of their land.

1829
The Winnebago are forced off their land.

1832
The Black Hawk War ends armed Native American resistance to U.S. settlers in Wisconsin.

1836
Wisconsin becomes a territory.

1600   **1700**   **1800**

1492
Christopher Columbus comes to New World.

1607
Capt. John Smith and three ships land on Virginia coast and start first English settlement in New World — Jamestown.

1754–63
French and Indian War.

1773
Boston Tea Party.

1776
Declaration of Independence adopted July 4.

1777
Articles of Confederation adopted by Continental Congress.

1787
U.S. Constitution written.

1812–14
War of 1812.

United States
History At-A-Glance

1848
Wisconsin becomes the thirtieth state to join the Union.

1849
Wisconsin gives African Americans the right to vote, but, because of problems counting votes, the right is not recognized as legal until 1865.

1854
The Republican Party is founded in Wisconsin.

1882
The first U.S. hydroelectric plant is opened in Fox River.

1890
Stephen M. Babcock develops a machine to test butterfat in milk, boosting dairy production.

1900
Robert La Follette becomes governor and brings many reforms.

1910
Victor Berger of Milwaukee is the first socialist elected to U.S. Congress.

1932
The nation's first unemployment compensation law is enacted in Wisconsin.

1939
Workers inadvertantly blast the face off an enormous cave that today is known as the Cave of the Mounds.

1959
The University of Wisconsin football fight song is adopted as the state's song.

1975
Menominee tribe gains federal recognition.

1996
Wisconsin Works program begins.

1800   **1900**   **2000**

1848
Gold discovered in California draws 80,000 prospectors in the 1849 Gold Rush.

1861–65
Civil War.

1869
Transcontinental Railroad completed.

1917–18
U.S. involvement in World War I.

1929
Stock market crash ushers in Great Depression.

1941–45
U.S. involvement in World War II.

1950–53
U.S. fights in the Korean War.

1964–73
U.S. involvement in Vietnam War.

2000
George W. Bush wins the closest presidential election in history.

2001
A terrorist attack in which four hijacked airliners crash into New York City's World Trade Center, the Pentagon, and farmland in western Pennsylvania leaves thousands dead or injured.

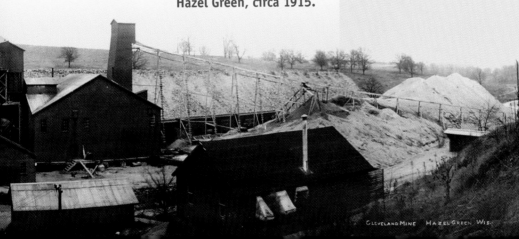

▼ The Cleveland Mine in Hazel Green, circa 1915.

Festivals and Fun For All

Check web site for exact date and directions.

EAA AirVenture, Oshkosh

Fighter jets, ultralight aircraft, vintage airplanes, and more are on display during AirVenture's annual two-week event in July. www.airventure.org

Country Jam USA, Eau Claire

One of three related country music festivals that take place throughout the United States. The event at Eau Clair takes place along the banks of the Chippewa River. www.countryjam.com

Summerfest, Milwaukee

Since 1968 Milwaukee has been home to what is one of the world's largest music festivals, featuring eleven days of live music by top performers, a variety of food, a carnival midway, and more. www.summerfest.com

American Birkebeiner, Hayward

In the year 1206, Norwegian warriors used Birkebeiner skis to travel hundreds of miles to reach a refuge for the eighteen-month-old son of the Norwegian king. Today the historic journey is reenacted in races that take place in Norway, Canada, and the United States. Wisconsin's American Birkebeiner is the largest cross-country ski race in North America. www.birkie.com/index1.html

Prairie Villa Rendezvous, Prairie du Chien

Every June, people come to southern Wisconsin to recreate the way people lived in the early 1800s. Reenactors perform Native American dances, demonstrate how to use nineteenth-century tools, teach basket weaving, and hold contests in archery and log-cabin cooking. The Rendezvous is also one of the biggest Native American trading events of the year. www.villageprofile.com/wisconsin/prairieduchien

▼ Summerfest.

The Great Circus Parade, Milwaukee

This recreation of a nineteenth-century circus parade is held annually. The parade, featuring seventy-five circus wagons, 750 horses, as well as other animals, marching bands, and clowns culminates at the parade showgrounds where circus perfomances can be seen under the Big Top.
www.circusparade.com

Door County Festival of Blossoms, Door County

Every spring, Door County bursts into bloom with thousands of wildflowers, daffodils, and cherry and apple blossoms. Celebrate with parades, contests, and wildflower walks.
www.doorcountyvacations.com

Lumberjack Bowl, Hayward

Lumberjacks and "lumberjills" compete as spectators flock to watch.
www.haywardfun.com/lwc

Spectacle of the Geese, Horicon

Thirty-one thousand acres (30 ha) of marshland provide a way station for more than two hundred thousand Canada geese on their annual southerly migration. The town holds a festival to celebrate the sight.
www.horiconchamber.com

Syttende Mai, Stoughton

The town of Stoughton celebrates its Norwegian heritage and the Seventeenth of May (Syttende Mai), Norwegian Independence Day.
www.stoughtonwi.com

World Championship Snowmobile Derby, Eagle River

Every January, snowmobile enthusiasts from around the world gather for races on Eagle River's ice track.
www.derbytrack.com/www/derbytrack

United States International Snow-Sculpting Competition, Milwaukee

Olympic winners and snow-sculpting teams from around the world compete to create the best snow sculptures on the last weekend in January.
www.travelwisconsin.com and click on "Cool Events"

The Warrens Cranberry Festival, Warrens

Every year, the bogs around Warrens — known as the Cranberry Capital of Wisconsin — bear about 285 million pounds (129,276,000 kg) of cranberries. The town has been celebrating this bounty since 1973.
www.cranfest.com

Wisconsin State Fair, West Allis

In 1851 a few Wisconsin farmers started the state fair as a way to exchange agricultural information among themselves. The fair celebrated its 150th birthday in 2001 and is still a popular event, now featuring everything from horse pulls to cream puffs.
wistatefair.com/static/sf2

Books

Anderson, William. *Pioneer Girl: The Story of Laura Ingalls Wilder.* New York: HarperCollins, 1998. A biography of the world-famous author of the Little House books.

Bromberg, Nicolette. *Wisconsin Revisited.* Madison, WI: State Historical Society of Wisconsin, 1998. A photographic portrait of one hundred fifty years in the life of Wisconsin.

Hieb, J. A, editor. *Visions and Voices: Winnebago Elders Speak to Children.* Independence, WI: Western Dairyland Economic Opportunity Council, 1994. Read the history that Winnebago (Ho-Chunk) elders have passed on to teens of their nation.

Holliday, Diane Young and Bobbie Malone. *Digging and Discovery: Wisconsin Archaeology.* Madison, WI: University of Wisconsin Press, 1997. Discover how much Wisconsin history can be found underground.

Lalicki, Tom. *Spellbinder: The Life of Harry Houdini.* New York: Holiday House, 2000. Find out more about this magical Wisconsinite.

Malone, Bobbie and Jefferson J. Gray. *Working with Water: Wisconsin Waterways.* Madison, WI: University of Wisconsin Press, 2001. Discover the many ways water has been involved in Wisconsin State history and economy, from glaciers to cranberry bogs.

Ostergren, Robert C. and Thomas R. Vale, editors. *Wisconsin Land and Life A Portrait of the State.* Madison, WI: University of Wisconsin Press, 1997. Learn more about Wisconsin history from early times to the present day.

Web Sites

▶ Official state web site

http://www.wisconsin.gov/state/home

▶ Official Madison web site

http://www.ci.madison.wi.us

▶ Wisconsin Historical Society web site

http://www.shsw.wisc.edu

▶ The American Memory Finder, part of the Library of Congress site, has a tremendous collection of primary source material, including downloadable photographs

http://memory.loc.gov/ammem/collections/finder.html

Note: Page numbers in *italics* refer to illustrations or photographs.